PERENNIALS

A QUANTUM BOOK

Published by Grange Books
an imprint of Grange Books Plc
The Grange
Kingsnorth Industrial Estate
Hoo, nr. Rochester
Kent ME3 9ND

ISBN 1-84013-268-X

This book is produced by
Quantum Books Ltd
6 Blundell Street
London N7 9BH

Project Manager: Rebecca Kingsley
Project Editor: Judith Millidge
Design/Editorial: David Manson
Andy McColm, Maggie Manson

The material in this publication previously appeared in
How to Plant and Grow Perennials

QUMSPPR
Set in Futura
Reproduced in Singapore by Eray Scan
Printed in Singapore by Star Standard Industries (Pte) Ltd

Contents

PERPETUAL PERENNIALS

Perennials have provided generations of gardeners with a wealth of colours, shapes, textures and sizes of plants and flowers, with bloom spanning the seasons from hellebores pushing through snow in winter to the hardiest of the chrysanthemums persisting into the chilly days of autumn. With many thousands of varieties available, the hardest part is usually narrowing down the choices.

Perennials in the Garden

The traditional way to use perennials is in borders, with the plants placed either in ribbon-like bands or in natural clumps. Except in very formal, geometric gardens, the latter method is generally preferred.

WHAT IS A PERENNIAL

Basically, it is a plant that lives more than two years, but as this would include trees and shrubs, further definition is required to eliminate these. Plants are herbaceous, having soft, fleshy stems that die back in autumn, though there are a few exceptions to this, such as ornamental grasses, semi-woody sub-shrubs and plants with ever-green foliage. While the foliage of most perennials dies each year, the roots can survive varying degrees of winter cold and send up new growth in the spring. A perennial may do this for several years, depending on many factors.

Left. Coreopsis verticillata, *Tickseed, is an ideal plant to brighten a meadow garden.*

Above. Violets and pansies can be used as ground cover or as an edging along paths.

USING PERENNIALS

Often two parallel borders are developed, where the plants are separated by a lawn, a path, or both. A fence, a hedge or wall is often included as a backdrop. Free-standing beds designed to be viewed from all sides is another way to use perennials. They can be used to underplant trees with shade-loving varieties, to produce a woodland garden.

Perennials native to alpine areas are the best ones to choose for softening the harsh lines of a stone wall or a rock garden, while perennials that tolerate moist, wet conditions can be planted beside a stream or pool to create a bog or marsh garden. A large lawn can be transformed into a glorious meadow garden when filled with brightly coloured flowers or ornamental grasses that thrive in these conditions.

Perennials, planted in pots or containers, turn a terrace or patio into a flower-filled retreat to afford hours of relaxation.

Ideal Growing Conditions

As you begin the process of deciding which perennials you want to grow, first take into account your growing conditions. These factors include a number of criteria which should be assessed before you start – minimum winter temperature, soil, light and water.

HARDINESS

This is mainly determined by the ability of a plant to survive a minimum winter temperature. Water and soil conditions also play a role. These work together so that even within a small garden, there will be such microclimatic differences that a plant may survive in one area but not in another. Good drainage is a key element, for should water be allowed to collect around roots and then freeze, the results are usually fatal. With experience you may be able to find that extra warm spot for growing a plant that is not usually hardy in your area.

Left. Hostas can turn a dull, shady garden into a wealth of texture and form.

Above. Mixing in taller plants near the front gives the border a dynamic look.

ASPECT

Although some perennials must have full sun, there are many that will tolerate either full sun or light shade, plus others that prefer light or even full shade. In regions with hot, humid summers, light or partial shade is often necessary for plants to survive. This can be provided by planting on the east or west side of a building, hedge or fence so that the sun is received for at least four to six hours each day. Very few perennials will bloom well in heavy dappled shade.

SOIL TYPE

Loam is the ideal soil for almost all perennials. It has a balanced mix of clay, sand, and silt particles, drains well, and has a generous supply of organic matter, or humus. It also enhances the growth of soil microorganisms that release plant nutrients. The most common sources of organic matter are peat moss, compost or leaf-mould. To assess drainage, dig a hole and fill with water. If the water has not seeped away in one hour, then you must assume that the drainage is poor.

Growing Perennials

For most people, choosing plants with low-maintenance qualities is of prime importance. However, there are certain chores which most gardeners have to perform to give young plants a good start, encourage reblooming or control the size of older more established plants.

SOIL PREPARATION

Proper preparation of the soil is necessary to bring lasting pleasure from your perennial garden. Use of a soil testing kit will familiarise you with the pH and nutrient levels in your garden. Wait until the soil is partially dry before digging and remove any large stones. Using a spade or fork, turn over the soil to a depth of 45cm (18in).

PLANTING PERENNIALS

Plants can be bought from garden centres and nurseries. Most plants will be old enough to bloom in the first year. Select plants that are bushy and compact, with healthy green foliage and no signs of damage or diseases. Plant out in late afternoon, on a cool and cloudy day, with rain predicted in a day or so. Avoid hot weather.

1. Prepare the soil well prior to planting.

2. Dig a hole large enough for the roots.

3. *Remove faded flowers and spent stems.*

4. *Dividing can create additional plants.*

PINCHING AND THINNING

Pinching out the growing tip from a plant forces side branches to grow readily, making plants shorter, sturdier, bushier and with more flowers. This is usually done before July on several occasions. Some perennials including delphiniums, phlox, Shasta daisies and asters, produce so many shoots that growth is spindly and circulation of air is poor, which will promote fungal diseases. Thinning out some of the stalks when they are 15cm (6in) tall will reduce this problem. Disbudding, removing some of the flower buds, allows the remaining bud to produce an extra large flower. Remove only the small side buds on hibiscus, peonies and large-flowered chrysanthemums.

DIVIDING PERENNIALS

As perennials grow and spread, each plant competes with itself and other plants for water, nutrients and space. Dividing perennials is needed either to rejuvenate an aging plant, to control the size of a plant or to have additional plants. Spring and summer blooming plants are usually divided in late summer or autumn and autumn blooming plants in early spring.

Water the bed well, several days before dividing plants. Using a fork or spade, dig up the entire clump. If possible, use your hands to divide the clump into smaller sections. Where the roots are tightly entwined, insert two forks back to back in the centre, press the handles together to prise the clump apart.

Developing a Design

Once you have established your growing conditions and considered the possible perennials, you are ready to develop a design. Borders are usually best if at least 1.2m (4ft) wide and beds 1.8m (6ft) at widest point.

A border will be viewed from many sides, so place taller plants at the back with shorter ones towards the front. With free-standing beds, place the tallest plants in the middle with plants of gradually decreasing heights towards the outer edges.

Placing some of the low-growing, spring-blooming plants towards the centre of a bed or border, can make a more interesting feature.

Observing when plants will flower in your area, as well as deciding how long a growing season you require, will help you to coordinate the plants for your garden. Using a colour wheel can help you plan a complementary colour schemes such as purple and yellow which can be very effective. While small plants in a compact garden and large plants in a big garden is recommended.

Below. Complementary colour schemes such as purple and yellow are popular.

Right. Schemes which use every colour available can be a challenge.

PERENNIAL SPECIES

Key to symbols

A number of icons are used throughout the directory to provide a snapshot of the idiosyncrasies of each species.

 Easy care

 Full sun

 Full sun to light shade

 Light shade

 Light to full shade

 Heat tolerant

 Cut Flowers

 Dried flowers

 Fragrant flowers

 Attract butterflies

 Meadow gardens

 Ground cover

 Rock gardens

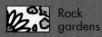 Bog gardens

THROUGHOUT THE DIRECTORY
The botanical name for each species is given first in alphabetical order, followed by the common name.

ACHILLEA MILLEFOLIUM YARROW

This can be an indispensable plant in gardens where low maintenance is a consideration. They are good for cutting and can be used fresh or dried. They have a tendency to become invasive in rich, moist soil.

Common name Yarrow.
Height 60cm (2ft).
Colour Yellow, red, pink, white.
Bloom time Early to midsummer.
Aspect Full sun.
Pests and diseases Gall, mildew and rust can be a problem.

ACONITUM CARMICHAELII MONKSHOOD

These are elegant plants with glossy leaves and wonderful spikes of unusually hooded blue flowers. Although used medicinally, all parts of this plant are poisonous and care should be taken with small children.

Common name Monkshood.
Height 90cm (3ft).
Colour Blue to violet.
Bloom time Mid to late summer.
Aspect Full sun to light shade.
Pests and diseases Crown rot, mildew, mosaic, or wilt may occur.

ADENOPHORA CONFUSA LADYBELLS

Resembling their close relatives, the campanulas, ladybells have delicate bell-like flowers. They do not transplant readily and should be planted in groups for the greatest effect.

Common name Ladybells.
Height 60cm (2ft).
Colour Yellow, red, pink, white.
Bloom time Early to midsummer.
Aspect Full sun to light shade.
Pests and diseases Gall, mildew and rust can be a problem.

ALCHEMILLA MOLLIS LADY'S MANTLE

This plant is a favourite with gardeners for its spreading mounds of velvety, rounded grey leaves with fan-like pleats and serrated edges. The frothy mass of flowers last several weeks and are delightful in fresh or dried bouquets.

Common name Lady's Mantle.
Height 30cm (12in).
Colour Yellow.
Bloom time Early to midsummer.
Aspect Full sun or light shade.
Pests and diseases Trouble-free.

AMSONIA TABERNAEMONTANA BLUE STARS

This low maintenance perennial has loose, rounded clusters of star-shaped flowers on stiff stems that provide a contrast to other stronger-coloured flowers. Good for cutting if the stems are seared to prevent 'bleeding'.

Common name Blue Stars.
Height 90cm (3ft).
Colour Pale blue.
Bloom time Spring to early summer.
Aspect Full sun to light shade.
Pests and diseases Trouble-free.

ANAPHALIS CINNAMOMEA PEARL EVERLASTING

Throughout summer small clusters of pearly white flowers provide material for dried flower arrangements. Cut when the flowers just begin to show their centres. It is one of the few silver or grey foliaged plants able to grow in moist soil.

Common name Pearl Everlasting.
Height 60cm (2ft).
Colour Pearly white.
Bloom time Early to midsummer.
Aspect Full sun to light shade.
Pests and diseases Gall, mildew and rust can be a problem.

ANCHUSA AZUREA BUGLOSS, ALKANET

Resembling Forget-Me-Nots, bugloss is favoured for the airy sprays of intensely coloured flowers which bloom over a long period. Preferring deep, humus-rich soil, these plants will have a second blooming if cut back after the first flowering.

Common name Bugloss.
Height 1.5m (5ft).
Colour Dark blue.
Bloom time Summer.
Aspect Full sun or light shade.
Pests and diseases Leafhoppers, mosaic.

ANEMONE x HYBRIDA JAPANESE ANEMONE

This is a diverse group of plants which include both perennials and bulbs, with some best suited for woodland or rock gardens.

Common name Japanese Anemone.
Height 90cm (3ft).
Colour Pink or white.
Bloom time Late summer to early autumn.
Aspect Full sun to light shade.
Pests and diseases Flea beetles, caterpillars, aphids, slugs, mosaic, rust.

ANTHEMIS TINCTORIA CAMOMILE

A daisy-like flower which is excellent for cutting and has ferny aromatic foliage. Tolerant of hot, dry conditions and sandy, slightly alkaline soil.

Common name Camomile.
Height 25cm (10in).
Colour Yellow.
Bloom time Late spring to early summer.
Aspect Full sun.
Pests and diseases Mildew can be a problem when air circulation is poor.

AQUILEGIA FLABELLATA COLUMBINE

An old favourite with unusually shaped early summer flowers. The cup and spur may be the same colour or in contrasting colours. Good for cutting, the flowers may be double.

Common name Columbine.
Height 38cm (15in).
Colour Bright blue.
Bloom time Early summer.
Aspect Full sun to light shade.
Pests and diseases Leaf miners, leaf spot, rust mosaic, aphids.

ARABIS CAUCASIA ROCK CRESS

A plant which produces creeping mounds of soft grey-green leaves and bears loose spikes of fragrant white flowers. May rot in hot, humid summers.

Common name Rock Cress.
Height 20cm (8in).
Colour White.
Bloom time Spring.
Aspect Full sun.
Pests and diseases Gall midge, club root, white blister, downy mildew.

ARMERIA MARITIMA THRIFT, SEA PINK

A plant with neat, grass-like clumps of evergreen leaves which bear leafless stalks with globe-shaped flower heads. These are excellent specimens for the rock garden, between flagstones, along walls, or at the front of a border.

Common name Thrift, Sea Pink.
Height 15cm (6in).
Colour Pink, cherry red, white.
Bloom time Spring to early summer.
Aspect Full sun.
Pests and diseases Trouble-free.

ARUNCUS DIOICUS GOAT'S BEARD

A handsome, large, shrubby plant for the back of the border, the centre of a bed or beside a pool. They bear feathery clusters of tiny flowers and have segmented leaves.

Common name Goat's Beard.
Height 1.5m (5ft).
Colour Creamy yellow.
Bloom time Early summer.
Aspect Light shade.
Pests and diseases Sawflies and in spring, caterpillars.

ASARUM EUROPAEUM WILD GINGER

These plants form a dense mat of shiny, heart-shaped leaves and are an excellent ground cover for shady areas. In mild regions, the foliage remains evergreen. The common name is derived from the aromatic scent of the foliage and roots when crushed.

Common name Wild Ginger.
Height 15cm (6in).
Colour Purple-brown.
Bloom time Spring.
Aspect Light to full shade.
Pests and diseases Slugs and snails.

ASCLEPIAS TUBEROSA BUTTERFLY WEED

These long-lived, easy-care plants are related to milkweeds and form similar canoe-shaped pods that are useful in dried flower arrangements. They are very variable as to flower shade and blooming time.

Common name Butterfly Weed.
Height 90cm (3ft).
Colour Orange, red or yellow.
Bloom time Midsummer.
Aspect Full sun.
Pests and diseases Trouble-free.

ASTER x FRIKARTII ASTER, MICHAELMAS DAISY

These are indispensable plants for the autumn, providing vibrant colour when other plants are yellowing. One of the few daisies which does not need staking, they also make excellent cut flowers.

Common name Aster, Michaelmas Daisy.
Height 1.8m (6ft).
Colour Blue, lavender, pink, red or white.
Bloom time Summer to autumn.
Aspect Full sun.
Pests and diseases Mildew, slugs, wilt, caterpillars, tarsonemid mites.

ASTILBE x ARENDSII ASTILBE

One of the most favoured, easily grown and long-lived perennials for shaded areas, it produces neat clumps of segmented, dark green leaves. The feathery spires of tiny flowers may be used for cutting.

Common name Astilbe.
Height 90cm (3ft).
Colour Pink, rose, red and white.
Bloom time Early to late summer.
Aspect Full sun to light shade.
Pests and diseases Trouble-free.

AUBRIETIA DELTOIDEA PURPLE ROCK CRESS

This plant forms a tall mat of downy, grey green leaves and thrives in full sun. It requires sandy, well-drained soil containing lime and a cool moist climate for best growth.

Common name Purple Rock Cress.
Height 15cm (6in).
Colour Purple, rose, red, lavender.
Bloom time Spring to early summer.
Aspect Full sun to light shade.
Pests and diseases Mildew, white blister.

AURINIA SAXATILIS GOLD DUST

Easily grown, this plant forms dense mounds of hairy grey-green leaves, covered in spring with tiny, bright yellow flowers. Often used as an edging to paths, at the front of a border, or spilling over a wall.

Common name Gold Dust.
Height 30cm (12in).
Colour Yellow.
Bloom time Early spring.
Aspect Full sun.
Pests and diseases Slugs, mildew, flea beetles, white blister.

BAPTISIA AUSTRALIS FALSE INDIGO

A lush, elegant, shrubby plant with sturdy, upright branching stems. The flowers are pea-like, and in early summer are followed by attractive seed pods. Never invasive, these plants are long-lived.

Common name False Indigo.
Height 1.2m (4ft).
Colour Deep blue.
Bloom time Early summer.
Aspect Full sun to light shade.
Pests and diseases Trouble-free.

BELAMCANDA CHINENSIS BLACKBERRY LILY

These plants resemble the iris with their thin, branching stalks bearing clusters of flowers. The flowers are marked by red-purple dots and when they fade, are replaced by seed pods, which open to reveal black seeds resembling blackberries.

Common name Blackberry Lily.
Height 75cm (30in).
Colour Yellow-orange.
Bloom time Midsummer.
Aspect Full sun to light shade.
Pests and diseases Iris borers.

BELLIS PERENNIS COMMON DAISY

Often grown as a biennial, the Common Daisy is useful as a spring accent for the border or rock garden. There are many varieties and colours, either as singles or doubles. They are happy growing in well-drained soil and need a winter mulch in very cold regions.

Common name Common Daisy.
Height 15cm (6in).
Colour Red, rose, pink, white.
Bloom time Spring to early summer.
Aspect Full sun to light shade.
Pests and diseases Trouble-free.

BELLIS / BELAMCANDA

28

BERGENIA 'ABENDGLUT' BERGENIA

This plant is grown both for its foliage and small flowers. Useful at the front of the borders, path edges and as ground cover under trees and shrubs. The leaves are often evergreen and used in flower arrangements.

Common name Bergenia.
Height 30cm (12in).
Colour Pink, magenta and white.
Bloom time Spring.
Aspect Full sun to light shade.
Pests and diseases Leaf spot.

CAMPANULA LACTIFLORA BELLFLOWER

One of the easiest bellflowers to grow, and hardy. The bell-shaped flowers are borne on long stiff spikes which appear in summer and may need staking. A loose mulch of oak leaves will help to protect plant crowns from winter injury.

Common name Bellflower.
Height 1.5m (5ft).
Colour Pale blue, violet blue, pink, white.
Bloom time Summer.
Aspect Full sun to light shade.
Pests and diseases Slugs, snails, froghoppers, wilt.

CENTAUREA MACROCEPHALA GOLDEN KNAPWEED, CORNFLOWER

These are an eye-catching species with strongly coloured, thistle-like or fringed flowers which are tolerant of neglect. They bloom for only a short time in midsummer.

Common name Golden Knapweed, Cornflower.
Height 1.2m (4ft).
Colour Bright yellow.
Bloom time Midsummer.
Aspect Full sun.
Pests and diseases Rust or mildew, in late summer, occasionally.

CENTRANTHUS RUBER RED VALERIAN

This species blooms for much of the summer with showy heads of small fragrant flowers. They are excellent as cut flowers and attract butterflies. They are bushy plants which are easily propagated and self-sow readily.

Common name Red Valerian.
Height 90cm (3ft).
Colour Yellow, red, pink, white.
Bloom time Summer.
Aspect Full sun to light shade.
Pests and diseases Trouble-free.

CERASTIUM TOMENTOSUM SNOW-IN-SUMMER

A popular plant which forms dense
mats of downy, silvery-grey, fine-textured
foliage and star-shaped pure white flowers.
Useful for planting in rock gardens, in
stone walls, as an edging, or as a ground
cover.

Common name Snow-in-Summer.
Height 15cm (6in).
Colour Pure white.
Bloom time Early summer.
Aspect Full sun.
Pests and diseases Trouble-free.

CHRYSANTHEMUM x MORIFOLIUM CHRYSANTHEMUM, DAISY

The daisy-like flowers of this species
can be single or double or pompons.
All colours have been developed. They
can be used singly, in groups, or
massed in borders, beds and rock
gardens, or used as an edging.

Common name Chrysanthemum,
Daisy.
Height 1.2m (4ft).
Colour All except blue.
Bloom time Late summer to autumn.
Aspect Full sun.
Pests and diseases Eelworm, leaf
miners, capsid bugs, red spider mites.

CLEMATIS INTERGRIFOLIA CLEMATIS

This solitary clematis has a sprawling growth habit, prominently veined leaves and bell-shaped flowers in midsummer.

Common name Clematis.
Height 1.2m (4ft).
Colour Lavender to violet-blue.
Bloom time Midsummer.
Aspect Full sun to light shade.
Pests and diseases Slugs, aphids, earwigs, powdery mildew, wilt, leaf spot.

COREOPSIS VERTICILLATA TICKSEED

The daisy-like flowers are very long-lasting, brightening up borders and meadow gardens for most of the summer.

Common name Tickseed.
Height 75cm (30in).
Colour Sunshine-yellow.
Bloom time Summer to autumn.
Aspect Full sun.
Pests and diseases Froghoppers, slugs.

DELPHINIUM LARKSPUR

Classic plants for the back of the border, well-known for their tall spikes of flowers, most often in shades of blue or purple. They do best in cool, moist climates, but can be grown elsewhere if expectations are lowered.

Common name Larkspur.
Height 1.8m (6ft).
Colour Blue, purple, white.
Bloom time Summer.
Aspect Full sun to light shade.
Pests and diseases Slugs, snails, crown, root and stem rot, powdery mildew, mosaic, wilt, grey mould.

DIANTHUS DELTOIDES CARNATION, PINKS

The fragrance of these plants is spicy and this has made them popular, in both the garden and as cut flowers, for centuries. The flowers are single, with the plants forming spreading mats of bright, semi-evergreen leaves.

Common name Carnation, pinks.
Height 15cm (6in).
Colour Pink.
Bloom time Early summer.
Aspect Full sun.
Pests and diseases Aphids, thrips, leaf spot, mildew, rust, wilt, grey mould.

DICTAMNUS / DICENTRA

DICENTRA SPECTABILIS BLEEDING HEART

Noted for their graceful shape and unusually formed flowers, these plants are popular for cottage, rock and wild flower gardens. They form a loose, open plant with divided leaves. Arching sprays of heart-shaped flowers emerge in late spring.

Common name Bleeding Heart.
Height 90cm (3ft).
Colour Rose-pink or pure white.
Bloom time Late spring.
Aspect Light to full shade.
Pests and diseases Trouble-free.

DICTAMNUS ALBA BURNING BUSH

A low maintenance, long-lived species which grows into a shrubby plant with glossy, dark green leaves. In summer, if a match is held near the flowers or seed pods, a flash of light will be produced from the ignition of the volatile oils given off by the plant.

Common name Burning Bush.
Height 90cm (3ft).
Colour White.
Bloom time Early summer.
Aspect Full sun to light shade.
Pests and diseases Trouble-free.

DIGITALIS PURPUREA FOXGLOVE

Tall spires of velvety flowers appear on this plant in early summer. They are useful as a vertical accent at the back of the border. In an informal garden they can be allowed to naturalise.

Common name Foxglove.
Height 1.2m (4ft).
Colour White or shades of pink or purple.
Bloom time Early summer.
Aspect Full sun to light shade.
Pests and diseases Crown and root rot in over wet ground.

DORONICUM CAUCASICUM LEOPARD'S BANE

Tidy, spreading mounds of glossy green, heart-shaped leaves make this plant a good specimen for the front of the border. The long-lasting flowers are daisy-like and prefer a humus-rich, moist, well-drained soil.

Common name Leopard's Bane.
Height 45cm (18in).
Colour Yellow.
Bloom time Late spring to early summer.
Aspect Full sun to light shade.
Pests and diseases Powdery mildew.

ECHINACEA PURPUREA PURPLE CONE FLOWER

This wild flower is excellent when massed in informal plantings, or as a bold specimen in the border. The cone flowers have coarse, hairy stems and leaves. The flowers are daisy-like and bloom over a long time.

Common name Purple Cone Flower.
Height 1.2m (4ft).
Colour Purple.
Bloom time Summer to autumn.
Aspect Full sun to light shade.
Pests and diseases Trouble-free.

ECHINOPS RITRO GLOBE THISTLE

This is an eye-catching plant for the middle or back of the border, popular for arrangements either dried or fresh. Globe-like clusters of tiny flowers are borne on branching stems. They are attractive to bees and moths.

Common name Globe Thistle.
Height 1.5m (5ft).
Colour Steel-blue.
Bloom time Summer.
Aspect Full sun.
Pests and diseases Trouble-free.

ERIGERON FLEABANE

Resembling asters, these plants have delicate, daisy-like flowers with yellow centres and are excellent for cutting. The plants are bushy and do best in sandy, well-drained soil.

Common name Fleabane.
Height 75cm (30in).
Colour Blue, pink, or white.
Bloom time Early to midsummer.
Aspect Full sun to light shade.
Pests and diseases Trouble-free.

ERYNGIUM SEA HOLLY

A striking, thistle-like plant with prickly blue-grey foliage and white or purplish, cone-shaped flowers. They are excellent for fresh or dried arrangements.

Common name Sea Holly.
Height 1.2m (4ft).
Colour Blue-grey.
Bloom time Summer.
Aspect Full sun.
Pests and diseases Trouble-free.

EUPATORIUM PURPUREUM JOE-PYE WEED, GRAVEL ROOT

The billowy clusters of tiny flowers, make this plant very attractive in beds or borders and meadow gardens. They are very attractive to butterflies and make good cut flowers.

Common name Joe-Pye Weed, Gravel Root.
Height 1.8m (6ft).
Colour Rose pink to purplish.
Bloom time Summer to autumn.
Aspect Full sun.
Pests and diseases Trouble-free.

EUPHORBIA EPITHYMOIDES SPURGE

These plants are characterised by their showy bracts, with very tiny flowers in the centre. Forming an evenly rounded mound, the bracts are golden yellow in spring. The leaves turn rose-coloured in the autumn. They do best in dry, sandy soil and readily self-sow.

Common name Spurge.
Height 30cm (12in).
Colour Yellow bracts.
Bloom time Spring.
Aspect Full sun.
Pests and diseases Grey mould.

FERNS

Ferns are at their best when massed under trees, along a wall or combined with spring-flowering bulbs. The leaves are superb as foliage in flower arrangements.

Common name Ferns.
Height 1.8m (6ft).
Colour Bright green.
Aspect Light shade to full shade.
Pests and diseases Slugs, snails, rust.

FILIPENDULA VULGARIS DROPWORT

These plants bring a fine texture to gardens with their lush, dark green leaves. The flowers are plumy, tiny clusters and are good for cutting, if picked before they are fully open. They readily self-sow.

Common name Dropwort.
Height 60cm (2ft).
Colour Yellow, red, pink, white.
Bloom time Early summer.
Aspect Full sun to light shade.
Pests and diseases Powdery mildew.

GERANIUM SANGUINEUM CRANE'S BILL

A plant which forms a mound with long-blooming, pink to magenta flowers. It is highly adaptable to various climates and also readily self-sows.

Common name Crane's Bill.
Height 45cm (18in).
Colour Pink to magenta.
Bloom time Spring to summer.
Aspect Full sun.
Pests and diseases Slugs.

GEUM 'MRS BRADSHAW' GEUM, AVENS

This plant forms low clumps of dark green leaves with thin, branching stems bearing flowers with wavy petals in summer. Moist soil and light shade are necessary

Common name Geum, Avens.
Height 60cm (2ft).
Colour Red, yellow or orange.
Bloom time Summer.
Aspect Full sun to light shade.
Pests and diseases Trouble-free.

HELIOPSIS HELIANTHOIDES FALSE SUNFLOWER

Vigorous, bold plants with dark green foliage and abundant clusters of golden daisy-like flowers, with slightly darker centres.

Common name False Sunflower.
Height 1.5m (5ft).
Colour Golden yellow.
Bloom time Summer to autumn.
Aspect Full sun.
Pests and diseases Trouble-free.

HELLEBORUS ORIENTALIS HELLEBORE

These are among the earliest perennials to flower. The nodding flowers, lasting a month or more, are able to withstand cold temperatures and snow.

Common name Hellebore.
Height 60cm (2ft).
Colour Yellow, red, pink, white.
Bloom time Late winter to spring.
Aspect Full sun to light shade.
Pests and diseases Leaf spot.

HEMEROCALLIS DAY LILY

Easily grown and widely adaptable, day lilies are very popular with many different hybrid varieties. Each flower lasts only one day, hence the common name, but a plant may produce dozens during a season.

Common name Day Lily.
Height 90cm (3ft).
Colour Yellow, orange.
Bloom time Summer to autumn.
Aspect Full sun to light shade.
Pests and diseases Trouble-free.

HESPERIS MATRONALIS SWEET ROCKET

This is a lovely cottage garden plant, resembling phlox, with wonderfully fragrant elongated clusters of flowers. Good for cut flowers, sweet rocket is short-lived, but readily self-sows.

Common name Sweet Rocket.
Height 90cm (3ft).
Colour Lavender, purple, mauve or white.
Bloom time Late spring to mid summer.
Aspect Full sun to light shade.
Pests and diseases Trouble-free.

HEUCHERA SANGUINEA CORAL BELLS

Coral bells produce a light, airy touch when planted in a rock garden or as an edging to a path. The bell-shaped flowers are produced on wiry stems, from low-growing clumps, and are good for cutting.

Common name Coral Bells.
Height 25cm (10in).
Colour Red, pink or white.
Bloom time Late spring through summer.
Aspect Full sun to light shade.
Pests and diseases Leaf gall.

HIBISCUS MOSCHEUTOS ROSE MALLOW, HIBISCUS

Exotic and bold, rose mallow makes a dramatic statement in the garden with its saucer-shaped flowers and broad leaves.

Common name Rose Mallow, Hibiscus.
Height 1.8m (6ft).
Colour White or shades of pink or red.
Bloom time Midsummer to autumn.
Aspect Full sun.
Pests and diseases Aphids, mealy bugs.

HOSTAS PLANTAIN LILY

One of the most widely used of all perennials, plantain lilies are chosen for their adaptability to various climates and soils. They are low-maintenance plants which form neat, symmetrical mounds of leaves of varying colours and textures.

Common name Plantain Lily.
Height 60cm (2ft).
Colour White, purple or lavender.
Bloom time Summer to autumn.
Aspect Light to full shade.
Pests and diseases Slugs.

IBERIS SEMPERVIRENS CANDYTUFT

One of the best spring-blooming plants, the white flowers are set off by the dense, finely-textured dark evergreen leaves. Excellent in rock gardens, tumbling over walls, as an edging, or in planters.

Common name Candytuft.
Height 25cm (10in).
Colour White.
Bloom time Spring.
Aspect Full sun.
Pests and diseases Flea Beetles.

IRIS IRIS

Irises have been a garden favourite for centuries. There are thousands of varieties in almost every colour except red. Flowers consist of three upright petals and three drooping petals and may be bi-coloured, with frilled or ruffled petals.

Common name Iris.
Height 75cm (30in).
Colour All except red.
Bloom time Spring to summer.
Aspect Full sun to light shade.
Pests and diseases Iris borer, soft rot.

KNIPHOFIA RED HOT POKER

Best used as individual accent plants or in groups of three in the front to the middle of beds or borders. The flowers are tubular on stiff spikes and bloom for a long period in midsummer.

Common name Red Hot Poker.
Height 75cm (30in).
Colour Red, orange, cream, coral or yellow.
Bloom time Midsummer to autumn.
Aspect Full sun.
Pests and diseases Thrips.

LAVANDULA ANGUSTIFOLIA LAVENDER

An old-fashioned garden favourite, lavender is beloved for its flowers and leaves. Effective as a specimen plant for borders and beds, the flowers can be used in fresh arrangements or dried for use in potpourri and sachets.

Common name Lavender.
Height 90cm (3ft).
Colour Purple, pink, white or lavender.
Bloom time Early to late summer.
Aspect Full sun.
Pests and diseases Froghoppers, leaf spot.

LINUM PERENNE FLAX

This plant forms a graceful, upright clump with small, fine-textured leaves and delicate-looking flowers. Each bloom last only a day, but if kept picked, plants will bloom all summer. Can be used in beds, borders and rock gardens.

Common name Flax.
Height 60cm (2ft).
Colour Blue, yellow or white.
Bloom time Summer.
Aspect Full sun.
Pests and diseases Trouble-free.

LOBELIA CARDINALIS CARDINAL FLOWER

Effective when planted beside streams, in meadow gardens, or lightly shaded beds and borders. Intensely coloured flower spikes will appear from summer to autumn, if growing conditions are correct.

Common name Cardinal Flower.
Height 1.2m (4ft).
Colour Scarlet red.
Bloom time Summer to autumn.
Aspect Light shade.
Pests and diseases Rhizoctonia, stem rot. A virus disease can occur.

LUPINUS x 'RUSSELL HYBRIDS' LUPIN

Lupins have showy spikes of pea-like flowers, with either solid or bi-colours. The bushy plants have hand-shaped leaves. The plants do not transplant readily once established and live for only four years.

Common name Lupin.
Height 90cm (3ft).
Colour Yellow, red, pink, white, blue, purple.
Bloom time Early summer.
Aspect Full sun to light shade.
Pests and diseases Crown or root rot, honey fungus, powdery mildew.

LYCHNIS CHALCEDONICA MALTESE CROSS

These plants form dense clumps of straight stems with hairy leaves and clusters of flowers. If faded flowers are removed, there will be a second blooming. Plants are short-lived but readily reseed.

Common name Maltese Cross.
Height 90cm (3ft).
Colour Orange-scarlet.
Bloom time Early to midsummer.
Aspect Full sun.
Pests and diseases Aphids, froghoppers. Can develop a virus disease.

LYTHRUM SALICARIA PURPLE LOOSESTRIFE

A very adaptable plant with a wide variation in colour and height. Low maintenance, bushy plants with small foliage, they provide texture in the garden with abundant flower spikes.

Common name Purple Loosestrife.
Height 90cm (3ft).
Colour Purple.
Bloom time Early summer to autumn.
Aspect Full sun.
Pests and diseases Trouble-free.

MACLEAYA CORDATA PLUME POPPY

This is best used as a specimen plant near a building or hedge. This is a bold and dramatic plant with rounded, scalloped blue-green leaves with silvery undersides. Fluffy plumes of petal-less flowers appear in summer, followed by attractive seed pods. Flowers and seed pods can be dried for arrangements.

Common name Plume Poppy.
Height 3m (10ft).
Colour Creamy-white.
Bloom time Summer.
Aspect Full sun to light shade.
Pests and diseases Trouble-free.

MARRUBIUM INCANUM HOREHOUND

Popular for the herb garden, this plant can also be considered for the flower borders and beds. It is one of the few silver-grey perennials which does not rot in hot, humid climates. Can be invasive, so remove flowers, unless self-sowing is desired.

Common name Horehound.
Height 90cm (3ft).
Colour White.
Bloom time Summer.
Aspect Full sun.
Pests and diseases Trouble-free.

MERTENSIA VIRGINICA VIRGINIA COWSLIP

A much loved spring-blooming flower, Virginia Cowslip is best grown in drifts under trees at the edge of the lawn. The foliage dies back in summer, so interplant with other plants. The flowers are funnel-shaped and fragrant and readily reseed.

Common name Virginia Cowslip.
Height 60cm (2ft).
Colour Blue.
Bloom time Spring.
Aspect Light to full shade.
Pests and diseases Trouble-free.

MONARDA DIDYMA BEE BALM

Long-lived and easily grown, the bee balm is adaptable, blooming for much of the summer. Excellent for cutting, the flowers attract bees. The dark green leaves have a minty scent, and both flowers and leaves can be dried to be used in potpourris.

Common name Bee Balm.
Height 90cm (3ft).
Colour White, pink, lavender, magenta, red or burgundy.
Bloom time Summer.
Aspect Full sun to light shade.
Pests and diseases Trouble-free.

NEPETA x FAASSENII CATMINT

Related to Catnip, Catmint has a delicate texture and an ability to blend readily with other flowers and plants. They produce sprawling mounds, useful for edging, in rock gardens or raised beds. The leaves are small, heart-shaped, and grey, densely covering the plants.

Common name Catmint.
Height 45cm (18in).
Colour Blue, white or pink.
Bloom time Spring to early summer.
Aspect Full sun.
Pests and diseases Powdery mildew.

OENOTHERA TETRAGONA EVENING OR MISSOURI PRIMROSE

The beautiful flowers, blooming for much of the summer, have made this plant popular for rock gardens or in beds or borders. They have shiny, green leaves and saucer-shaped flowers. The seed pods can be dried for bouquets.

Common name Evening or Missouri Primrose.
Height 60cm (2ft).
Colour Yellow.
Bloom time Summer.
Aspect Full sun.
Pests and diseases Eelworms, root rot, mildew.

PAEONIA PEONY

These are among the most widely grown of perennials and will live for decades. The bushy plants have lush, shiny foliage and although best left undisturbed, can be divided in autumn, cutting roots apart with a knife.

Common name Peony.
Height 90cm (3ft).
Colour White, pale yellow, pink, red.
Bloom time Late spring to early summer.
Aspect Full sun.
Pests and diseases Honey fungus, swift moth caterpillars, leaf spot, wilt.

PAPAVER ORIENTALE ORIENTAL POPPY

An old-fashioned favourite, the Oriental poppy is good for cutting if picked, just as the buds are beginning to open. The leaves are fern-like, silver-green and rough-textured. As the plants go dormant after flowering, they should be planted in beds or borders, near other perennials.

Common name Oriental Poppy.
Height 1.2m (4ft).
Colour Orange, red, pink, salmon, white.
Bloom time Early summer.
Aspect Full sun.
Pests and diseases Downy mildew.

PENNISETUM ALOPECUROIDES FOUNTAIN GRASS

This plant has typical grassy foliage with an abundance of fuzzy, bottle-brush flowers that are green in mid summer, changing to brown in autumn, and tan in winter.

Common name Fountain Grass.
Height 75cm (30in).
Colour Green.
Bloom time Midsummer.
Aspect Full sun.
Pests and diseases Trouble-free.

PHLOX PANICULATA GARDEN PHLOX

Growing in clumps, this plant blooms from summer to early autumn with large, open clusters of flowers. They can be temperamental, susceptible to mildew, and do best in cool-summer areas.

Common name Garden Phlox.
Height 1.2m (4ft).
Colour Pink, white, red, pale blue.
Bloom time Summer to early autumn.
Aspect Full sun to light shade.
Pests and diseases Eelworms, slugs, leaf spot, leafy gall, powdery mildew.

PHYSOSTEGIA VIRGINIANA OBEDIENT PLANT

Easy to grow, this plant forms bushy clumps with wand-like spikes of tubular flowers. The flowers are excellent for cutting. Spreading rapidly, this is a useful plant in wild flower gardens and beside streams.

Common name Obedient Plant.
Height 1.2m (4ft).
Colour Pink, magenta, rose lilac, white.
Bloom time Summer to autumn.
Aspect Full sun.
Pests and diseases Trouble-free.

PLATYCODON GRANDIFLORUM BALLOON FLOWER

Forming stiffly, bushy plants, balloon flower derives its common name from the shape of the bud, which opens into a star-shaped flower. A long-blooming perennial with many varieties. Flowers are beautiful in arrangements; stem ends must be seared in a flame.

Common name Balloon Flower.
Height 75cm (30in).
Colour Blue, white or pink.
Bloom time Summer.
Aspect Full sun to light shade.
Pests and diseases Trouble-free.

POLYGONATUM ODORATUM THUNBERGII SOLOMON'S SEAL

The different forms of Solomon's seal are all similar in appearance, with arching, unbranched stems of pointed, oval leaves and drooping, tubular, white or cream flowers. The rhizamatous roots spread slowly forming handsome colonies.

Common name Solomon's Seal.
Height 90cm (3ft).
Colour Creamy white.
Bloom time Late spring to early summer.
Aspect Light to full shade.
Pests and diseases Trouble-free.

PRIMULA DENTICULATA PRIMROSE

The primrose has rounded heads of lilac flowers. Forming ground-hugging clumps with long, narrow or rounded, oval leaves and clusters of five-petalled, semi-double, or double flowers. Although they are generally short-lived, primroses are readily started from seed.

Common name Primrose.
Height 25cm (10in).
Colour Lilac.
Bloom time Spring.
Aspect Full sun to light shade.
Pests and diseases Aphids, brown core, caterpillars, grey mould, rust.

PULMONARIA SACCHARATA BETHLEHEM SAGE

These form small creeping plants with hairy, semi-evergreen, mottled leaves with grey or white spots. The clusters of flowers may be white, blue or pink.

Common name Bethlehem Sage.
Height 45cm (18in).
Colour White, blue or pink.
Bloom time Spring.
Aspect Full sun to light shade.
Pests and diseases Sawfly.

RUDBECKIA FULGIDA BLACK-EYED SUSAN

Forming a tall, bushy plant with hairy leaves, black-eyed Susan has yellow-orange flowers surrounding a brown-black cone. The flowers are good for cutting, and the dark cones remaining after the flowers fade, are eye-catching in the winter garden.

Common name Black-Eyed Susan.
Height 90cm (3ft).
Colour Yellow-orange.
Bloom time Summer to autumn.
Aspect Full sun.
Pests and diseases Slugs, snails.

SALVIA x SUPERBA VIOLET SAGE

The longest-lived perennial sage and easy to grow. The plant produces an abundance of flowers which are good for fresh or dried arrangements. Deadhead regularly to prolong the blooming period and winter mulch.

Common name Violet Sage.
Height 90cm (3ft).
Colour Dark purple.
Bloom time Summer.
Aspect Full sun.
Pests and diseases Red spider mites.

SCABIOSA CAUCASICA SCABIOUS, PINCUSHION FLOWER

Flowers stalks are produced from clumps of finely cut, grey-green foliage. The textured flowers are excellent for cutting and look their best when planted in groups of three near the front of beds and borders.

Common name Scabious, Pincushion Flower.
Height 45cm (18in).
Colour Blue, lavender-blue or white.
Bloom time Summer to autumn.
Aspect Full sun.
Pests and diseases Slugs, snails, mildew.

SEDUM 'AUTUMN JOY' STONECROP

This is the most widely grown stonecrop. The leaves are grey-green and the clusters of tiny flowers start in early autumn. These can be dried or left on for landscape interest in the winter.

Common name Stonecrop.
Height 60cm (2ft).
Colour Pale pink to salmon rose-red.
Bloom time Early autumn.
Aspect Full sun.
Pests and diseases Rust.

SMILACINA RACEMOSA FALSE SOLOMON'S SEAL

This plant has arching stems of pointed oval leaves resembling Solomon's seal. The flowers are feathery clusters of tiny creamy-white blooms, that become clusters of bright red berries in late summer. A good foliage plant which spreads by rhizomatous roots.

Common name False Solomon's Seal.
Height 60cm (2ft).
Colour Creamy-white.
Bloom time Spring.
Aspect Light to full shade.
Pests and diseases Trouble-free.

SOLIDAGO GOLDEN ROD

Forming a broad, upright clump with branching, graceful golden-yellow flowers, golden rod can be stunning if planted in groups of three. The flowers are good for fresh arrangements or can be dried and preserved in glycerine for winter bouquets.

Common name Golden Rod.
Height 1.1m (42in).
Colour Golden-yellow.
Bloom time Summer to autumn.
Aspect Full sun.
Pests and diseases Caterpillars, mildew.

STACHYS MACRANTHA BIG BETONY

The leaves of this plant are large, hairy, wrinkled, dark green and heart-shaped. The flowers appear on whorled spikes from late spring. The flowers can be used for cutting.

Common name Big Betony.
Height 60cm (2ft).
Colour Violet, lavender-pink, rosy-pink.
Bloom time Late spring to early summer.
Aspect Full sun to light shade.
Pests and diseases Rot can occur in hot, humid climates.

STOKESIA LAEVIS STOKES' ASTER

This aster produces a stiff, branching plant with long, narrow leaves that are evergreen in warmer climates. The flowers are lacy, fringed and excellent for cutting. It is at its best when planted in groups of three at the front of the border.

Common name Stoke's Aster.
Height 60cm (2ft).
Colour Blue or white.
Bloom time Summer to autumn.
Aspect Full sun.
Pests and diseases Trouble-free.

THALICTRUM FLAVUM MEADOW RUE

These plants have a fine-textured, elegance for the back of the borders and beds. The fluffy, yellow flowers are good for cutting.

Common name Meadow Rue.
Height 1.5m (5ft).
Colour Yellow.
Bloom time Spring to summer.
Aspect Full sun to light shade.
Pests and diseases Trouble-free.

THERMOPSIS VILLOSA CAROLINA THERMOPSIS

These plants resemble lupins with their long spikes of pea-like flowers on stout stalks. Plants will eventually form clumps. These are long-lived plants, able to survive neglect, with attractive foliage all summer long and drought-resistant roots.

Common name Carolina Thermopsis.
Height 1.5m (5ft).
Colour Yellow.
Bloom time Early to midsummer.
Aspect Full sun.
Pests and diseases Trouble-free.

TRADESCANTIA x ANDERSONIANA SPIDERWORT

Forming robust clumps, this plant has long, narrow, grass-like leaves. There are clusters of three-petalled flowers at intervals along the stems. Each flower lasts a day, but blooming continues throughout the summer.

Common name Spiderwort.
Height 75cm (30in).
Colour Blue, pink, mauve, maroon, rose-purple or white.
Bloom time Summer.
Aspect Full sun to light shade.
Pests and diseases Slugs.

VERONICA TEUCRIUM SPEEDWELL, VERONICA

A somewhat sprawling plant, the flowers appear in late spring. The plants have narrow, dark green, toothed leaves. They are long-lived plants in well-drained soil.

Common name Speedwell, Veronica.
Height 30cm (12in).
Colour Navy blue.
Bloom time Summer.
Aspect Full sun.
Pests and diseases Powdery mildew.

VIOLA TRICOLOR HEARTSEASE

These diminutive plants have been grown for centuries. They are popular in wild gardens and as ground cover. The stems are sprawling and the plant short-lived but the readily reseeds.

Common name Heartsease.
Height 30cm (12in).
Colour Tri-coloured purple, yellow and white.
Bloom time Spring to early summer.
Aspect Full sun to light shade.
Pests and diseases Mosaic, leaf spot, rust.

Index Alphabetical listing of botanical names.

I N D E X

Index
Alphabetical listing of common names.